Super Suzi
and the
Cat Burglar

Super Suzi

She's a
schoolgirl and
a superhero.
She always gets
home in time
for dinner.

The Cat Burglar

He's a robber
who climbs like a
cat. He'll take your
things – and drink
all your milk!

by Carmel Reilly

illustrated by Mike Moran

OXFORD
UNIVERSITY PRESS
AUSTRALIA & NEW ZEALAND

Suzi was walking home from school.

Stop, robber!

5

The Cat Burglar ran around a corner.

I can't see him!

Is that him up there?

8

WHOOSH!

Never say never, Cat Burglar!

I've got you!

STR-E-TCH

M-I-A-O-W!

Suzi rang the police …

… and took the bag back.

Thank you, Super Suzi!

You're going to go to JAIL for a long time!

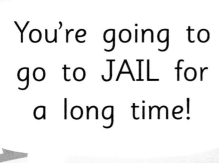

I'll be back, Super Suzi!

Suzi went home ...

I'm just in time for dinner!

15

Retell the Story

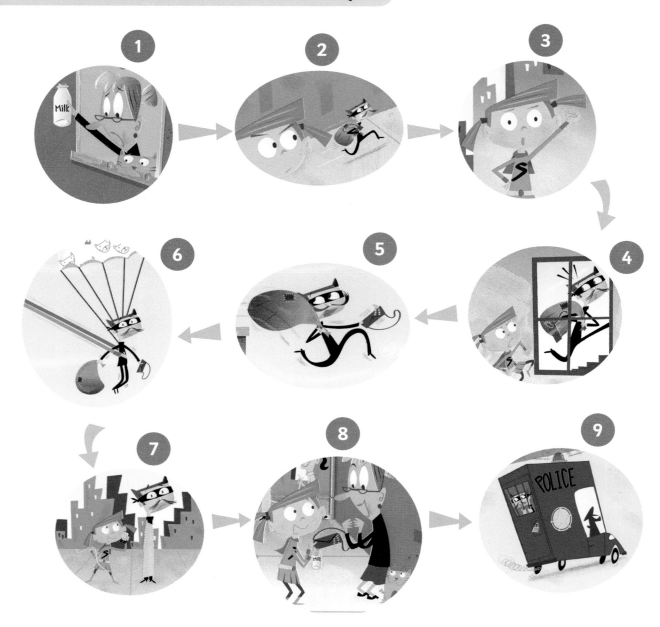